DESTINY OF DOOM

TITAN
C O M I C S

LEGO® GRAPHIC NOVELS AVAILABLE FROM TITAN™

NINJAGO #1 (on sale now)

NINJAGO #2 (on sale now)

NINJAGO #3 (on sale now)

NINJAGO #4 (on sale now)

NINJAGO #5 (on sale now)

NINJAGO #6 (on sale now)

NINJAGO #7 (9 Jan 15)

NINJAGO #8 (9 Jan 15)

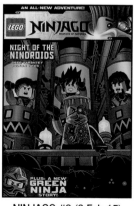

NINJAGO #9 (6 Feb 15)

TITAN COMICS

#8 DESTINY OF DOOM

GREG FARSHTEY • Writer
JOLYON YATES • Artist
LAURIE E. SMITH • Colourist

TITAN
COMICS

LEGO® NINJAGO™ Masters of Spinjitzu
Volume Eight: Destiny of Doom

Greg Farshtey – Writer
Jolyon Yates – Artist
Laurie E. Smith – Colourist
Bryan Senka – Letterer

Published by Titan Comics, a division of Titan Publishing Group Ltd., 144 Southwark St., London, SE1 0UP. LEGO NINJAGO: VOLUME #8: DESTINY OF DOOM. LEGO, the LEGO logo, the Knobs and Brick configurations and Ninjago are trademarks of the LEGO Group ©2014 The LEGO Group. All rights reserved. All characters, events and institutions depicted herein are fictional. Any similarity between any of the names, characters, persons, events and/or institutions in this publication to actual names, characters, and persons, whether living or dead and/or institutions are unintended and purely coincidental. License contact for Europe: Blue Ocean Entertainment AG, Germany.

A CIP catalogue record for this title is available from the British Library.

Printed in China.

First published in the USA and Canada in May 2013 by Papercutz.

10 9 8 7 6 5 4 3 2 1

ISBN: 9781782761990

www.titan-comics.com

www.LEGO.com

MEET THE MASTERS OF SPINJITZU...

JAY

COLE

ZANE

KAI

LLOYD

And the Master of the Masters of Spinjitzu...

SENSEI WU

It has been a month since the defeat of the Stone Warriors. Peace has returned to the world of Ninjago...

But the Ninja know they must keep training, just in case trouble strikes again...

NOW, JAY, I'LL--

HA! KAI, DID YOU EXPECT ME TO WAIT FOR IT?

LET'S SEE HOW YOU LIKE THE PYTHON THROW, AND-- →OOF!←... COME ON-- WHY ISN'T THIS WORKING?

MAYBE YOU'RE DOING IT WRONG?

THEY HAVE ACCOMPLISHED MUCH, MY NINJA... BUT THEY STILL HAVE MUCH TO LEARN.

WELL, THEY HAVE AN EXCELLENT TEACHER, MY BROTHER.

PERHAPS I HAVE TAUGHT THEM ALL I KNOW. THEY WOULD BENEFIT FROM A NEW INSTRUCTOR.

ME? WHAT COULD I TEACH THEM, OTHER THAN HOW TO BRING MISERY?

YES, YOU WERE A DESTROYER, ONCE...

NOW YOU HAVE THE CHANCE TO BE A BUILDER. THE CHOICE IS YOURS.

I TRY AND TRY AND I JUST CAN'T MASTER THAT MOVE!

THERE MUST BE SOME SIMPLE TRICK I AM MISSING.

THERE IS. YOU HAVE TO DROP YOUR RIGHT SHOULDER AS YOU MOVE IN SO YOU CAN GET THE RIGHT LEVERAGE.

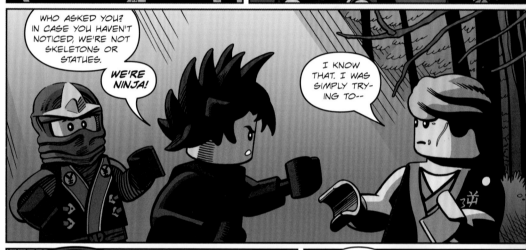

WHO ASKED YOU? IN CASE YOU HAVEN'T NOTICED, WE'RE NOT SKELETONS OR STATUES.

WE'RE NINJA!

I KNOW THAT. I WAS SIMPLY TRY-ING TO--

DON'T. JUST DON'T. AFTER ALL YOU'VE DONE, YOU'RE CRAZY IF YOU THINK WE'LL LISTEN TO YOU!

KAI, COME ON. BACK OFF.

I DON'T BLAME YOU FOR HOW YOU FEEL, KAI.

MAYBE MY BEING HERE AT ALL IS A MISTAKE.

Later...

IS THIS TRULY WISE?

MAYBE NOT. BUT IT'S SOMETHING I HAVE TO DO.

I KNEW THERE WAS ALWAYS A CHANCE MY PLANS TO CONQUER NINJAGO MIGHT FAIL. SO I CRAFTED ONE LAST PLOT, TO BE ACTIVATED IF I WAS DEFEATED.

AND WHEN YOUR CORRUPTION WAS BANISHED AND YOU RETURNED TO NORMAL--

IT WILL SEE THAT AS MY DESTRUCTION AND LAUNCH AUTOMATICALLY. THAT'S WHY I HAVE TO GO AND STOP IT... *ALONE.*

NOT ALONE, DAD. I'M COMING WITH YOU.

WE DIDN'T GET BACK TOGETHER ONLY TO BE SEPARATED AGAIN SO SOON.

WHATEVER YOU HAVE TO FACE, I WILL FACE WITH YOU.

AND WE'RE GOING ALONG TOO-- OR DID YOU THINK WE TRUSTED YOU ALONE WITH ONE OF YOUR SUPER-WEAPONS?

KAI!

THERE'S NO TIME TO ARGUE. BUT UNDERSTAND, I CANNOT PROMISE ANY OF US ARE GOING TO COME BACK.

WE'LL TAKE THAT CHANCE.

KAI HAS A POINT. YOU DESIGNED THAT THING-- WHAT IS ITS WEAK SPOT?

YOU'RE RIGHT, COLE, I DESIGNED IT... SO IT DOESN'T HAVE A WEAK SPOT.

WELL, WE CAN'T JUST STAND HERE!

NO. LET US ENDEAVOR TO BRING THE CRAFT DOWN.

NNNIIINNNJJJAAAAOO!

As if sensing a threat, the disc begins to spin at high speed.

The sudden surge in air pressure blows the Ninja away...

And slams them to the ground...

WHOOOM

WELL ÷OUCH!÷ THAT WENT WELL.

WE HAVE TO FOLLOW THAT THING-- FIND SOME WAY TO DESTROY IT.

AND WE WILL.

WHAT IS THAT?

CALL IT AN IGNITION KEY.

A LITTLE SOMETHING I PICKED UP IN THE MOUNTAINS OF MADNESS.

MY CREATION COULD START AUTOMATICALLY... OR I COULD START IT.

BUT CAN YOU STOP IT?

I CAN BRING US TO WHERE IT IS HEADING. THE REST WILL BE UP TO US.

PREPARE YOUR-SELVES--

--FOR THE NEXT BATTLE.

HEY! HOW DID YOU DO THAT?

22

WAIT, WHAT'S IT DOING NOW?

Before the startled eyes of the Ninja, the disc and the giant figure fuse together to form one menacing object...

HISSSSSSSS

THIS HAS GONE FAR ENOUGH!

KAI, WAIT!

DON'T GET TOO CLOSE, OR--

NO--!

UH-OH...

SPUN TOO NEAR... COLE, KAI-- GO LIMP! DON'T FIGHT BACK!

I TAKE ORDERS FROM THE SENSEI, NOT FROM YOU!

YOU LITTLE FOOL! YOU ARE GOING TO DO WHAT I SAY, BECAUSE I AM NOT GOING BACK TO WU CARRYING YOUR BODY.

DO YOU UNDERSTAND ME?

OH, WHY NOT?

I CAN'T PUT A DENT IN THIS THING ANYWAY. WE'RE GOOD AND TRAPPED.

ZANE! JAY! LLOYD! GET READY-- YOU MAY HAVE TO MOVE FAST!

STAY STILL, COLE.

THE UPDRAFT FROM MY WHIRLWIND WILL HELP YOU SAFELY TO THE GROUND.

CAUGHT YOU, DAD!

I NEVER DOUBTED YOU WOULD.

UM, THANKS... I MEAN... ÷URK÷

...I'M AFRAID YOU'RE A LITTLE HEAVIER THAN... ÷UNNGH÷

...THAT IS, I THINK I MIGHT

--DROP YOU! DAD!

÷OOF!÷

WAM

ARE YOU OKAY?

I... WILL BE, LLOYD. THANK YOU.

30

OKAY, BUT HE'S NOT LIKE THAT ANYMORE. HE COULDN'T BE. RIGHT, DAD?

SON, YOU KNOW I WAS CORRUPTED AS A YOUTH BY THE BITE OF THE GREAT SERPENT.

AND I HAVE NOW PURGED THAT CORRUPTION, BUT... WHO KNOWS?

DID THE SERPENT'S BITE CAUSE MY EVIL, OR DID IT SIMPLY BRING TO THE SURFACE WHAT WAS ALREADY THERE?

THERE, THAT PROVES IT! LEAVE HIM HERE AND WE'LL BREAK HIS TOY ON OUR OWN.

KAI, YOU'RE NOT HELPING EVEN MORE THAN USUAL. NOW I HAVE QUESTIONS AND GARMADON HAS ANSWERS--

SO PIPE DOWN AND LET ME ASK THEM.

HOW WAS IT BUILT, WHAT DOES IT DO, AND WHY DID YOU SCREAM WHEN YOU REMEMBERED IT?

IT WAS BUILT BY SAMUKAI AND MYSELF IN THE UNDERWORLD, PRIOR TO THE SKELETON ARMY'S ATTACK ON NINJAGO.

AND WHEN HE HEARD THE WORDS, HE REMEMBERED THE WEAPON... PAINFULLY. BUT THAT BRINGS US NO CLOSER TO STOPPING IT.

MAYBE, MAYBE NOT. GARMADON, DID YOU BUILD ALL THE PIECES YOURSELF?

THREE OF THEM, YES, WITH SAMUKAI'S AID. THE LAST PIECE HE BUILT HIMSELF, FROM MY PLANS.

THEN WE MIGHT HAVE A CHANCE! LET'S GO, GUYS, THIS FIGHT'S FAR FROM OVER!

~:BRRRRR!:~ HOW COME EVIL MASTERMINDS NEVER HIDE THEIR WEAPONS SOMEPLACE WARM?

THEY'RE NOT TRYING TO MAKE IT EASY, THAT'S WHY.

THEN THEY SUCCEED AT NOT TRYING.

YOU STILL HAVEN'T EXPLAINED HOW THIS THING IS GOING TO DESTROY THE WORLD.

IT WILL ACTIVATE THE MAGMA LAYERS BENEATH THE PLANET'S SURFACE. THE RESULTING LAVA FLOWS WILL OBLITERATE EVERY LIVING THING ON NINJAGO.

WE ARE EARLY. IT WILL TAKE TIME FOR THE REST OF THE MACHINE TO ARRIVE. MAYBE WE CAN USE THAT TO OUR ADVANTAGE.

HOW?

WE GET THE NEXT PIECE... BEFORE IT GETS US.

So begins a massive effort to dig beneath the thick ice to get to the next piece of Garmadon's weapon...

KRAKK

Once holes are made in the surface, the Ninja use Spinjitzu to drill tunnels beneath the ice...

Until at last, one Ninja breaks through to -- what?

At first, the Ninja are too stunned to say anything. Then, finally...

LOVE YOURSELF MUCH?

EVERY MAN WANTS TO LEAVE A LEGACY BEHIND.

HUH. I THOUGHT THAT WAS ME.

DIFFERENT KIND OF LEGACY, LLOYD, UNLESS YOU CAN MAKE MAGMA ERUPT TOO.

SNAP

ENOUGH TALK. DESTROY THIS... ABOMI-NATION.

For the next few hours, Garmadon and the Ninja bash, batter, and beat the giant metallic "head," trying to wreck it while there is still time. But their efforts produce no result.

Or do they...?

BUILT TO LAST, I'LL SAY THAT. WHAT IS THAT THING MADE OUT OF?

METAL FORGED IN THE UNDERWORLD.

WHAT NOW, FEARLESS LEADER?

SIMPLE. IF WE CAN'T BEAT IT, WE BURY IT. WE'LL BRING THIS CAVERN DOWN ON TOP OF IT.

HEY, GUYS, THAT'S A GREAT IDEA AND ALL, BUT... I DON'T THINK THE BIG HEAD LIKES IT.

NO, HE DOESN'T LIKE IT AT ALL!

SSHAKOW

HISSSSSS

SCATTER!

I'M A FOOL! THE TIME WE WASTED ATTACKING THAT THING GAVE THE REST OF THE MACHINE TIME TO GET HERE.

BEAT YOURSELF UP LATER. HOW ARE WE GOING TO STOP THAT?

YEAH, AND BEFORE IT STOPS US?

ZZZZAAKK

HEY, LET'S USE THE OLD "ICE MIRROR" TRICK! WE'LL REFLECT THE BEAMS RIGHT BACK AT IT. THAT NEVER FAILS!

Minutes pass...

I DON'T THINK IT'S COMING BACK UP.

MAYBE IT SHORT-CIRCUITED.

AT LEAST WE STOPPED IT FROM FLYING OUT TO JOIN THE REST OF THE MACHINE.

WAIT. DO YOU HEAR THAT?

HEAR WHAT? REMEMBER, YOUR EARS ARE BETTER THAN OURS.

EVERYONE, GET OFF THE LEDGE-- GET AWAY FROM THE WALL! *NOW!*

WHAT IS IT? WHAT'S HAPPENING?

THRAKKK THRAKKK

I HAVE A FEELING I KNOW, BUT I'M NOT SURE I BELIEVE IT.

GET READY! HERE IT COMES!

41

THAT SETTLES IT.

THE NEXT TIME GARMADON WANTS TO GO DO SOMETHING BY HIMSELF, I SAY LET HIM.

EVERYBODY ON THEIR FEET. WE'VE GOT A FIGHT ON OUR HANDS.

UM, SPEAKING OF HANDS...

THAT HEAD WEIGHS TONNES. MAYBE IT'S OFF-BALANCE-- HIT IT!

44

I THINK I'LL CHECK IN ON ZANE.

CAN'T BE FUN BEING ALONE WITH A GIANT MECHANICAL GARMADON.

OF COURSE, IF THAT PIECE OF JUNK SUDDENLY WAKES UP, TWO OF US WON'T BE ABLE TO STOP IT ANY MORE THAN ONE COULD.

YIKES!

I'M NOT GOING TO FIGHT YOU, KAI.

THEN THIS IS GOING TO BE A REALLY SHORT BATTLE.

RAISE YOUR HANDS! DEFEND YOURSELF!

NO.

KAI, STAND DOWN. THAT'S AN ORDER.

FINE. I HAVE TO TAKE CARE OF THE GIANT VERSION OF HIM FIRST, ANYWAY.

THANK YOU.

YOU'RE RIGHT. THE ONLY CHANCE WE HAVE IS IN THE NEXT BATTLE... NOT THIS ONE.

IT WOKE UP ABRUPTLY... THERE WAS NO WARNING.

THEN IT WASN'T DEAD. IT WAS JUST RECHARGING.

THIS IS THE FINAL SITE. WE WIN HERE, OR WE DON'T WIN.

FROM ICE FIELD TO TROPICAL JUNGLE... ONE THING ABOUT BEING A NINJA, IT'S REALLY HARD TO KNOW WHAT TO PACK.

WE DON'T HAVE FAR TO GO.

WE'LL MAKE CAMP AND GET READY. GARMADON AND I HAVE A PLAN WE THINK... WE HOPE... MIGHT WORK.

IF IT DOESN'T INVOLVE GETTING HALF-BURIED IN ICE CHUNKS AGAIN, I'M IN.

WE'LL ALL DO WHAT WE HAVE TO, COLE. NO MATTER WHAT.

GOOD, BECAUSE I DON'T THINK YOU'RE GOING TO LIKE WHAT'S ASKED OF YOU.

That night...

SO WE'RE AGREED?

YES. OUR LAST, BEST OPPORTUNITY MAY BE WHEN THE MACHINE IS WHOLE, STRANGE AS THAT MIGHT SOUND.

PROBABLY. EVERY PART THAT YOU DESIGNED SEEMS TO BE INVULNERABLE. SAMUKAI DESIGNED THE LAST PART. I'M HOPING HE'S NOT THE ENGINEER YOU ARE.

NOW I HAVE A QUESTION FOR YOU... WHY DID YOU LET US COME ALONG? YOU COULD HAVE WALKED THROUGH ONE OF YOUR GATES AND DISAPPEARED WHENEVER YOU LIKED.

MAYBE I FELT I NEEDED TO PROVE SOMETHING TO LLOYD, TO THE REST OF YOU... AND TO MYSELF.

NOT TO ME, DAD. NEVER TO ME.

COLE, IF YOU DON'T MIND, I'D LIKE TO TALK TO MY DAD.

I'M GOING TO GET SOME SLEEP. I THINK TOMORROW IS GOING TO BE A LONG DAY FOR US ALL.

And it seems Cole is right, for even now, Garmadon's machine knifes through the skies of Ninjago...

Can it think about its mission? Can it question its orders? No. It is just a weapon.

But perhaps, in some way, it can feel... for it was born from anger and fear, and that is all it has ever known...

If true, things are much worse than the Ninja think-- for then it would be a weapon that can feel rage for its targets.

KABLAM

Maybe, this time, Garmadon finally went too far...

The next morning, Garmadon leads the Ninja to a strange site: a tar pit in the centre of the jungle.

WELL, I HAVEN'T SEEN ANYTHING LIKE THIS BEFORE.

INDEED. IT CANNOT BE A NATURAL FEATURE OF THIS AREA.

IT'S NOT. SAMUKAI AND I CREATED IT TO HIDE THE FINAL PIECE.

SO WE GO DOWN THERE AND GET IT.

YOU WOULDN'T LAST A MINUTE, KAI. THIS STUFF IS BOILING HOT.

THE FOURTH PIECE WON'T EMERGE UNTIL THE REST OF THE MACHINE GETS HERE.

WHEN IT DOES, ZANE AND I WILL GO TO WORK-- THE REST OF YOU WILL BACK US UP.

WHY LEAVE THE OTHERS BEHIND?

ZANE IS THE ONLY ONE WHO CAN DO HIS PART OF THIS JOB. IT'S ALL PART OF THE PLAN.

SO ALL WE GET TO DO IS WATCH?

WATCH AND HOPE... WHILE MY DAD IS RISKING HIS LIFE SO WE CAN HANG ONTO OURS.

SO IT'S OUR EASIEST MISSION, OR OUR LAST, TAKE YOUR PICK.

ONCE THE ENGINE IS ATTACHED, IT BECOMES THE SOLE POWER THAT ALLOWS THE MACHINE TO FLY.

IF I CAN DISABLE IT, THEN MAYBE--

NO. THERE CAN'T BE ANY MAYBE.

I OWE THIS TO LLOYD. I OWE THIS TO NINJAGO.

IT SHOULD BE EASY. JUST WHIRL INSIDE, FIND THE RIGHT WIRE, PULL IT, AND GET OUT IN A MATTER OF SECONDS.

AND IF I DON'T GET OUT... MAYBE IT WOULD BE NO MORE THAN I DESERVE.

ALL RIGHT, ENOUGH BROODING. JUST GET INSIDE AND DO YOUR JOB AND--

YOWWW!

ZZZAAPP

YIIIIIIIIIIII!

SAMUKAI! HE BOOBY-TRAPPED THE ENGINE!

NOW I WILL HAVE TO SPINJITZU INSIDE WITHOUT TOUCHING THE SIDES.

I DON'T CARE. LET THE WHOLE THING BE A DOOM TRAP--

I WILL DO WHAT MUST BE DONE!

NOW IF ONLY HE HASN'T CHANGED THE WIRING PANEL...

BECAUSE IF HE HAS, I MAY HAVE LOST FOR THE FINAL TIME.

4.9 SECONDS UNTIL THE NEXT FLAME BURST, GARMADON.

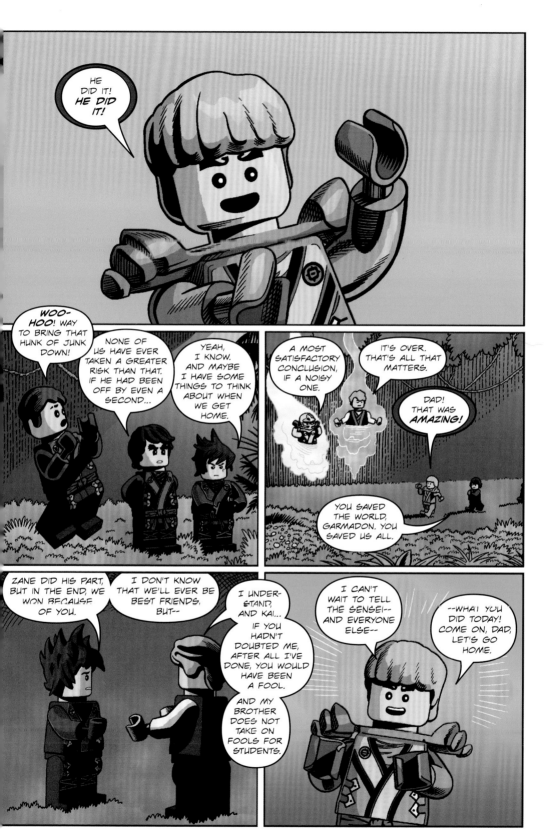

NO, LLOYD, I'M SORRY. I WON'T BE GOING BACK WITH YOU.

WHAT? BUT, DAD, THERE'S NO REASON FOR YOU TO--

YOU HAVE NOTHING LEFT TO PROVE TO ANYONE, IF THAT'S WHAT YOU--

IF IT'S ABOUT ALL THE THINGS I SAID--

IT'S NOT ABOUT ANY OF YOU. IT'S ABOUT ME. IT'S ABOUT WHO I AM... AND WHO I WAS.

I DON'T UNDER-STAND.

AS I WAS BRINGING DOWN THAT...

...THAT MONSTROSITY, I WAS THINKING WHAT A TERRIBLE WASTE OF TIME IT WAS TO BUILD IT IN THE FIRST PLACE.

AND THEN I REALISED THAT THE SAME COULD BE SAID OF MY LIFE.

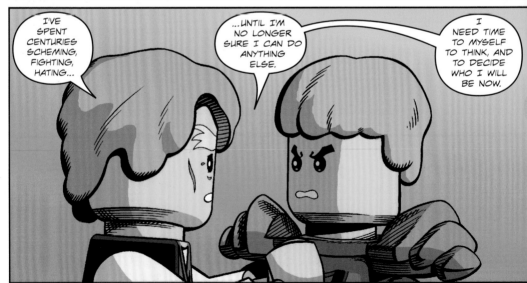

I'VE SPENT CENTURIES SCHEMING, FIGHTING, HATING...

...UNTIL I'M NO LONGER SURE I CAN DO ANYTHING ELSE.

I NEED TIME TO MYSELF TO THINK, AND TO DECIDE WHO I WILL BE NOW.

THE END.

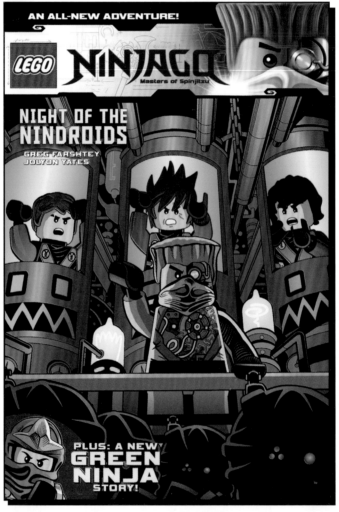